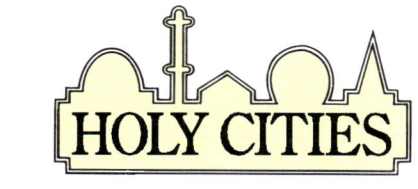

HOLY CITIES

KYOTO

Richard Tames

Evans

Evans Brothers Limited

Published by Evans Brothers Limited
2A Portman Mansions
Chiltern Street
London W1M 1LE

© copyright in the text and illustrations
Evans Brothers Limited 1995

British Library Cataloguing in Publication Data.
A catalogue record for this book is available from the British
Library.

First published 1995

Printed in Hong Kong by Wing King Tong Co. Ltd

ISBN 0 237 51458 3

ACKNOWLEDGEMENTS

Editorial: Catherine Chambers
Design: Sally Boothroyd
Production: Jenny Mulvanny

The author and publishers would like to thank: Saviour
Pirotta for his help in devising the Holy Cities series and Dr
John Breen, of the School of Oriental and African Studies,
University of London, for his help on this book.

Maps: Jillian Luff of Bitmap Graphics

For permission to reproduce copyright material the author
and publishers gratefully acknowledge the following:

Front cover: Main photograph – Hein shrine, Kyoto, Frank
Leather, Trip; inset left – Japanese tea ceremony in Court
costume, Frank Leather, Trip; inset right – Priest at prayer in
the Eiheiji Temple, Toyofumi Mori, The Image Bank

Back cover: Prayer plaques at shrine, Richard Tames

Endpapers: Front – The Golden Pavilion is probably Kyoto's
most famous building – Frank Leather, Trip; Back – The
giant carts used in Kyoto's annual Gion Festival weigh
about 20 tonnes each and are difficult to move – Frank
Leather, Trip

Title page: Tori Gates, Fushimi Inari, Paul Harris, Royal
Geographical Society

Contents page: Yatuko Nomae ceremony, Yasaka shrine,
Kyoto, Paul Harris, Royal Geographical Society

page 6 – P Rauter, Trip; page 7 – Spectrum Colour Library;
page 8 – e.t. archive; page 9 – M Malintyre, The Hutchison
Library; page 10 – (left) B Lovell, Spectrum Colour Library,
(right) M Rivas Micoud, Life File; page 11 – Richard Tames;
page 12 – Paul Harris, Royal Geographical Society; page 13 –
David Ball, Spectrum Colour Library; page 14 – Tokyo
National Museum, Life File; page 15 – Jeremy Hoave, Life
File; page 16 – e.t. archive; page 17 – B Lovell, Spectrum
Colour Library; page 18 – (top) PM Field, Trip, (bottom)
Richard Tames; page 19 – (top) Martin Barlow, Trip,
(bottom) Richard Tames; page 20 – Richard Tames; page 21
– e.t. archive; page 22 – (top) Jeremy Hoave, Life File,
(bottom) Paul Harris, Royal Geographical Society; page 23 –
Richard Tames; page 24 – Richard Tames; page 25 – Paul
Harris, Royal Geographical Society; page 26 – Robert
Harding Picture Library; page 27 – (top) Richard Tames,
(bottom) Jon Burbank, The Hutchison Library; page 28 –
Richard Tames; page 29 – Frank Leather, Trip; page 30 –
Paul Harris, Royal Geographical Society; page 31 – S
Burman, The Hutchison Library; page 32 – Spectrum Colour
Library; page 33 – Spectrum Colour Library; page 34 – (top)
Frank Leather, Trip, (bottom) M Barlow, Trip; page 35 –
Frank Leather, Trip; page 36 – Richard Tames; page 37 –
(top) Brett Froomer, The Image Bank, (bottom) M Rivas
Micoud, Life File; page 38 – (top) Trip, (bottom) Paul Harris,
Royal Geographical Society; page 39 – (top) e.t. archive,
(bottom) Jeremy Hoave, Life File; page 40 – Robert Harding
Picture Library; page 41 – (left) Robert Francis, Robert
Harding Picture Library, (right) Tokyo National Museum,
Life File; page 42 – (top) M MacIntyre, The Hutchison
Library, (bottom) e.t. archive; page 43 – Paul Harris, Royal
Geographical Society; page 44 – The Image Bank

Contents

The meanings of the words in **bold** can be found in the **Key word** boxes at the end of each chapter.

Kyoto, the heart of Japan

An ancient capital

Kyoto was built on a flat plain, overlooked by towering mountains and cut by winding rivers. The city was the capital of Japan for over a thousand years, from 794 until 1868. It is thought to be Japan's greatest cultural centre, and contains some of the country's most beautiful gardens and buildings. Many of them were made for followers of Japan's two main religions – Shinto and Buddhism. In Japan, most people follow both religions, and thousands of worshippers come to visit Kyoto's Shinto **shrines** and Buddhist temples.

A place to visit

Kyoto was not just a capital and a major centre of religion but also a great place of learning. It still has one of Japan's most important Buddhist colleges at Enryakuji Temple. The city has always been Japan's leading home of traditional crafts, and the arts of tea ceremony and flower arranging (see pages 39 to 40).

Today, Kyoto is a modern city, with glass and concrete skyscrapers, but tourism still plays a major part in the city's life. Although Kyoto has suffered from many great fires over the centuries, it was not destroyed by bombing during World War Two. Visitors come to see the graceful old shrines and temples that other parts of Japan have lost. Kyoto has almost 2,000 places of worship for tourists and **pilgrims** to choose from. Some visitors just want to stroll in the beautiful shrine and temple gardens. Others come to buy locally-made souvenirs, such as brightly-patterned silk or **enamelled** jewellery.

Many school parties go to Kyoto to visit historic places such as Nijo castle or the palaces built for the emperor and his **courtiers.** Almost every tour organised for

▲ *The hills surrounding Kyoto*

tourists from abroad includes a stop in Kyoto. More than 38,000,000 people visit the city every year.

Modern Kyoto also has factories for making electrical goods, chemicals and machinery. As well as this there are 37 universities and colleges and 24 museums. The most important is Kyoto National Museum, which has 202 items that are so precious they are called 'National Treasures'. There are only about a thousand 'National Treasures' in the whole of Japan. Many Japanese people would agree that Kyoto itself is Japan's greatest 'National Treasure.' To many Japanese, it is known as '*Hana no Miyako*' – the Flowering Capital.

Key words

shrines places where a particular god or gods are worshipped

pilgrims people who travel to a holy place

enamelled decorated with shiny, coloured decoration set into metal

courtiers high-ranking people who act as friends and servants to an emperor

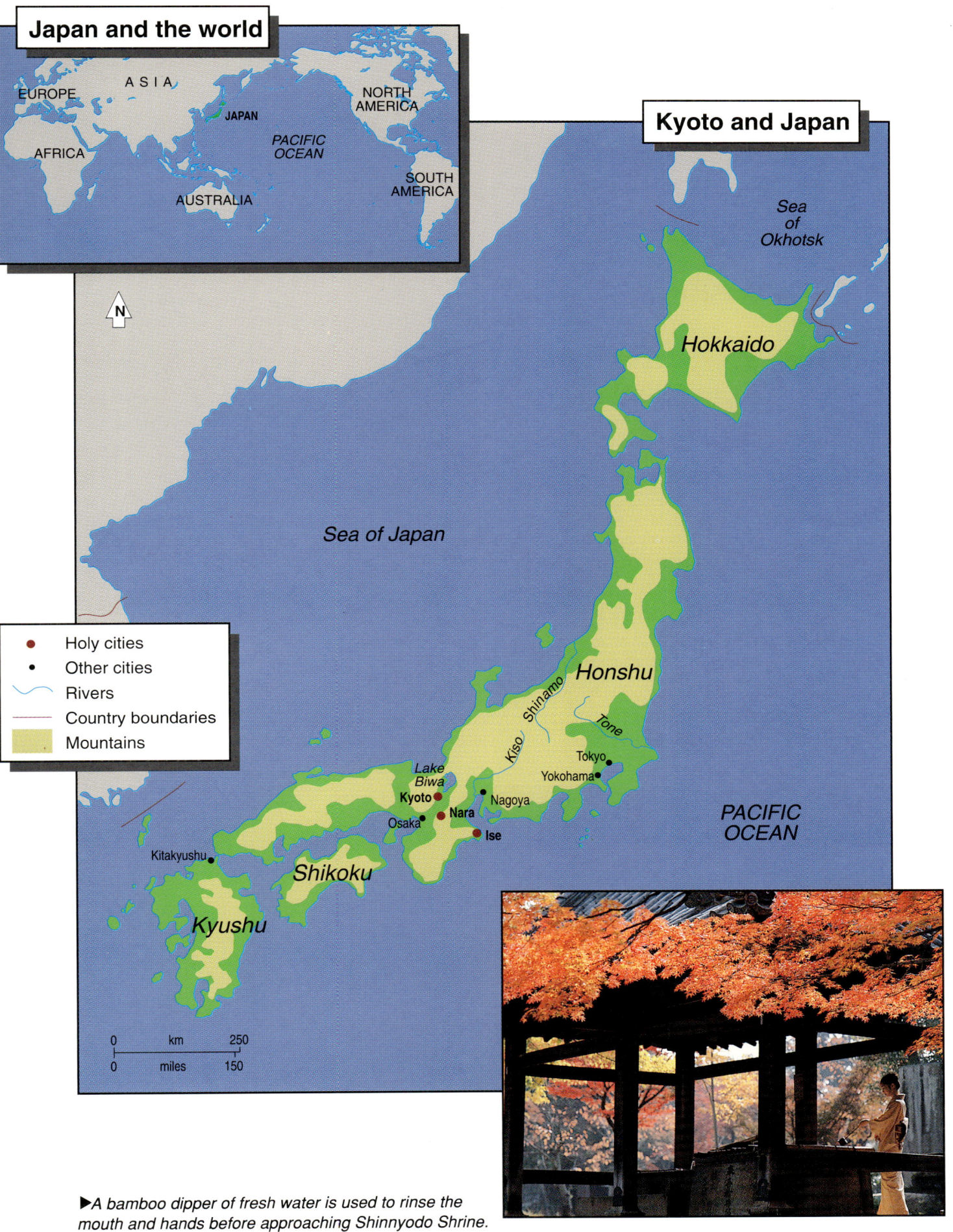

Japan and the world

EUROPE

A S I A

NORTH AMERICA

JAPAN

AFRICA

PACIFIC OCEAN

AUSTRALIA

SOUTH AMERICA

Kyoto and Japan

N

Sea of Okhotsk

Hokkaido

Sea of Japan

Honshu

Kiso Shinamo

Tone

Tokyo

Yokohama

Lake Biwa

Kyoto

Nagoya

Osaka

Nara

Ise

Kitakyushu

Shikoku

PACIFIC OCEAN

Kyushu

- ● Holy cities
- ● Other cities
- ～ Rivers
- — Country boundaries
- ▨ Mountains

| 0 | km | 250 |
| 0 | miles | 150 |

▶A bamboo dipper of fresh water is used to rinse the mouth and hands before approaching Shinnyodo Shrine.

How Japan began

In ancient times almost every people had stories to explain how they thought their community began. These stories are called myths, and they often became part of a people's religion because they were usually about a god or gods.

The Sun Goddess hides herself

It is said that all of Japan's emperors are **descended** from Amaterasu, the Sun Goddess. In one story, Amaterasu became angry with her naughty younger brother, Susanoo, and hid in a cave. While she hid there, the world was completely dark. The other gods had a party with music and dancing. This was to get Amaterasu to come out of the cave and make the world bright again. Amaterasu was curious when she heard the noise and came out of the cave to join in the fun. So the sun shone again.

Today, Japan's national flag is a red disc on a white background. The flag is called *hinomaru*, which means 'circle of the sun'.

It reminds people of the legends that surround Amaterasu, and her importance to the emperors of Japan.

An emperor for Japan

Later, Amaterasu sent her grandson, Ninigi, to conquer the Japanese islands. She gave him three treasures to show that he was the ruler – a sword, a mirror and a jewel. All emperors of Japan to this day have been given a sword, mirror and jewel to show that they are the rightful ruler.

According to legend, Ninigi's grandson, Jinmu, became Japan's first emperor. Tradition says that he began to reign in 660 BC after he had conquered the Yamato area of central Honshu, Japan's main island, with the help of a golden bird. The emperors of Yamato have always reigned in Japan, although their advisors, and **shoguns**, have often had the real power.

▼ *This Japanese wood block print shows Amaterasu, the Sun Goddess. In this myth, she is emerging from the earth.*

▲ Traditionally, a swordsmith's forge was a sacred area. Japanese blades were of excellent quality and lasted for centuries.

Royal tombs

Jinmu may never have existed. But the **ancestors** of the present emperor possibly began to rule the Yamato area around the 4th century AD, although many people think it was later than this. Archaeologists have dug up many huge mounds called *kofun*, which were made as tombs for members of the ruling family. Some tombs were round, some square and some were shaped like a keyhole. Even the smallest *kofun* are 15 metres across.

The biggest tomb is said to be that of Emperor Nintoku, who lived around 400 to 450 AD. It is 486 metres long and surrounded by a moat and a wood. Altogether it covers 32.3 hectares. Apart from the bodies of important people, these tombs also contained rich treasures, such as weapons, pots, harnesses and tools, to be used in the life after death. There are also many pottery figures called *haniwa*, which act as guardians or servants of the dead.

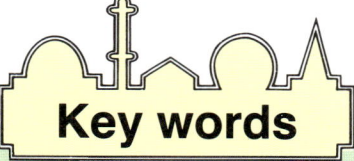

Key words

descended describes how a person comes from past members of their family

BC the years before the birth of Christ

shoguns warlords who ruled in the name of the emperor

ancestors past members of a person's family

AD the years after the birth of Christ

Think and do

1 The sun is very important in the myths and traditions of many peoples. Can you name any sun gods or goddesses from other cultures and religions?

2 Why do you think that the sun is an important symbol of power?

Shinto – Japan's first religion

Shinto is a religion that is only found in Japan. It means 'the way of the gods'. Unlike most other religions Shinto has no official **founder**, no set beliefs and no **scriptures**. It does have many festivals, ceremonies and rituals. Kyoto has hundreds of Shinto shrines.

Kami

Shinto began as a way of thanking the gods for the beauty of nature and the fertility of the land. In **prehistoric** times the people of Japan believed that *kami* (gods) lived in each mountain, tree, lake or rock. The sun, moon, earth, wind and sky were also *kami*.

Offerings of food, such as rice and salt, were left out for the *kami* in the hope that they would make sure there was a good harvest. The Japanese emperor still makes such offerings every year, for the whole nation. Festivals (*matsuri*) connected with farming are also an important part of Japanese life.

As the emperors of the Yamato region became more powerful, they acted as priests, leading ceremonies to worship the *kami*. Dances (*kagura*) were performed and music was played. Emperors, great warriors, scholars and poets were also worshipped as *kami* after they died.

▲ *A painting of the Shinto god of wind*

Festivals and prayers

Shinto ceremonies celebrated life, birth and the harvest (see page 12). Death and disease were believed to be **polluting**. People who came into contact with them came to shrines to make themselves pure again. This might involve saying prayers, making offerings, **fasting** or even standing under a holy waterfall. Pilgrims offered valuable things, such as swords, armour or cloth.

When a person visits a Shinto shrine nowadays they stop at the entrance (*torii*) to rinse out their mouth and wash their hands with fresh, clean water. It is important to be

◀ *Ladles for washing at the entrance of Jindaiji Temple*

clean before worship begins. Then they go up to the altar, clap twice and say a short prayer to thank the god of the shrine or ask for a favour.

In the past, most homes had a small altar in their best room where offerings could be made to the *kami*. This protected the house and the family who lived in it. Nowadays this is not so common in the cities, although many homes in the countryside still have altars.

Ise

The most famous of all Shinto shrines is not in Kyoto but at Ise (see map on page 7). It is said that Ise is the home of the Sun Goddess, Amaterasu. Japanese people have been going on pilgrimage to Ise for a thousand years. The Ise priests used to promise followers that if they went to Ise at least seven times they were certain to go to heaven when they died. Nowadays, people are more likely to go to Ise to see the unusual **architecture**.

▶ *Looking up into a Shinto shrine, where white streamers hang as a sign of purity. The bells are rung to wake up sleeping kami (gods), so that they listen to people's prayers.*

▼ *A* torii *gateway marks the approach to a Shinto shrine*

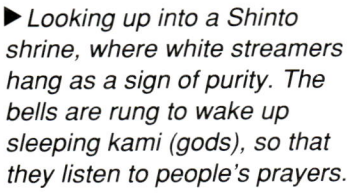

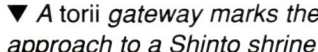

▲ Hundreds of prayer tablets at a shrine

Always new

Every 20 years, the Inner Shrine is rebuilt nearby and the old one is knocked down. It is rebuilt in exactly the same style as the old one, but with new wood. The reason for rebuilding is that Shinto respects things that are clean and pure. The shrine is never put up on exactly the same spot. This way, there is always a complete shrine standing.

The Outer Shrine is said to be the home of the god of food, clothing and housing. It is also knocked down and rebuilt regularly.

Festivals

Ise's most important festival is held every October to give thanks for the rice harvest. There is another ceremony at the beginning of each year to pray that the harvest will be a good one. Food is offered to the gods in bowls which are made in a kiln at the shrine. After they have been used they are thrown away. The food for the gods is grown in special places and cooked over a fire made by rubbing sticks together until they burst into flame.

Home of the Sun Goddess

There are two shrines at Ise – the Inner Shrine, which is said to date from the 3rd century AD, and the Outer Shrine, said to date from the 5th century AD. The Ise shrines are mentioned in a book of poems written in the 8th century, so they are definitely more than 1100 years old.

The Inner Shrine is the legendary home of the Sun Goddess, Amaterasu. Her symbol is a sacred mirror. This is one of three treasures given to an emperor at his **enthronement**. The main building is designed in a style that is not allowed for any other shrine. It is probably like the storehouses built in prehistoric times for rice and treasures. The building is raised off the ground on pillars to protect its contents from the damp.

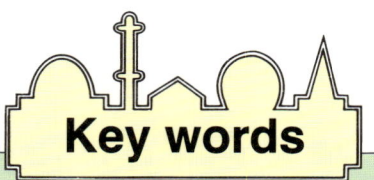

Key words

founder a person who begins something

scriptures holy writings

prehistoric the time before historical records were kept

polluting making dirty or unhealthy

fasting going without food on purpose

architecture the style of a building

enthronement the ceremony at which someone becomes an emperor or monarch

Buddhism comes to Japan

The Buddha

Buddhism is the name of the religion founded by an Indian prince called Gautama, who was born in Nepal around 500 BC. When he was 29 he gave up living in luxury and left his family to travel. He wanted to find out the purpose of life and how he should live. He studied with wise and holy men. For six years he suffered great poverty, fasting so much that he nearly died. Then he realised that punishing himself was as bad as giving himself too much. The middle path, having neither too much nor too little, was the best path to follow.

Gautama spent many years in **meditation** before he finally made up his mind about the purpose of life and how he should live. He spent the rest of his days preaching to followers who became **monks** and spread his teachings. He preached his first **sermon** at Sarnath, in India. Buddhist monks shaved their heads, did not marry or own property and often lived by begging.

After Gautama died, his followers called him Buddha, which means 'someone who has woken up to the truth'. Buddha's teachings were written down as scriptures known as *sutras*. Buddhists believe that there were other Buddhas, but Gautama is the most honoured.

▶ *A Japanese Buddhist monk*

What Buddha taught

Buddha believed that all life involved confusion and suffering. People suffered because they were greedy and wanted to hold on to things, including life. He believed that living things were endlessly reborn after death. The only way to reach final peace was to escape the cycle of rebirth so that no spark of life remained to be reborn. This could only be achieved by living a truly just and balanced life, as the Buddha himself had learned to do. He gave his followers a guide, to show them how to stop greed and hatred. The guide is known as *The Four Noble Truths*.

One of the most important duties for Buddhists was to show kindness towards all living things. This is because each one contains a soul, which has the chance to escape from the cycle of rebirth and achieve perfect peace. Lying, stealing, killing, drinking alcohol, trying to do magic spells and making **sacrifices** were all forbidden to followers of Buddhism.

Buddhists were also taught that they should do only good things because bad deeds can harm people and other living things. Buddha Gautama asked his followers to make five promises to help them to do good in the world.

The spread of Buddhism

Buddhism spread eastwards from India, both south to Sri Lanka, Burma and Thailand and north to China and Korea. Over the centuries, the scriptures were studied by many wise people. They were translated from the languages in which they were originally written, Pali and Sanskrit, into Chinese and other languages. This gave more people a chance to study them.

As the scriptures try to explain some very difficult and unusual ideas, **scholars** sometimes disagreed with one another about what they meant. These disagreements led Buddhists to form different groups, called sects. Each sect had its own beliefs and ways of worshipping.

▲ *Japanese fan-shaped Buddhist scriptures*

A new religion for the emperor

According to tradition, about a thousand years after Buddha died, the king of Paekche in Korea sent a gold statue of the Buddha and some books about Buddhism to the Japanese emperor, Kinmei. The emperor's advisors argued over the new religion. Kinmei and the powerful Soga family wanted to learn more about the new faith. But a group of courtiers led by the Mononobe family said that the Shinto gods would be angry and bring disaster to the country. As if to prove their point a plague broke out. The Buddha statue was thrown in a canal. But the quarrel went on until the Soga family almost wiped out the Mononobe in a battle. So this new religion of peace was taken up by the court as a result of a **massacre**!

Buddhism becomes Japanese

In 594 AD the powerful Prince Shotoku ordered that Buddhism should be taught to everyone. He brought over more Buddhist teachers from China and Korea and sent Japanese to study there. He built a number of **monasteries** to train monks who went out and preached the new religion. The oldest surviving one is at Horyuji. It contains the oldest wooden buildings in the world. Buddhism spread among the Japanese people when the monks taught them that they could become Buddhists without having to give up Shinto. At the end of the 8th century AD, a famous Japanese teacher, Kobo Daishi, explained Shinto and Buddhism in a new way. He called the new faith *Ryobo Shinto*, 'the Shinto of Two Kinds'.

By the time Buddhism came to Japan from China, it had become a very complicated religion. Buddhists believed that Buddha had taken on many different forms and had all sorts of spirits and messengers to help him. They guarded his temples and looked after his followers. Some of these helpers were *bodhisattvas* – people who had lived such good lives that they could have become Buddhas themselves. Instead of becoming Buddhas, they were so sorry for other people's suffering that they chose to wait until everyone else in the world could become Buddhas too.

Buddhism seemed to have lots of different gods – just like the Shinto *kami* (gods). Japanese scholars believed that Shinto *kami* were Buddhist gods, but in a Japanese form. The two kinds of gods worked together to help and protect ordinary people.

Buddhist temples and Shinto shrines were often built side by side in the same grounds. In their homes, people had altars for both Buddhist and Shinto worship. Buddhist priests looked after Shinto shrines, but often brought in their own ornaments, **images** and **rituals**.

▶ *A Japanese stone statue of Buddha Gautama, with offerings of food*

Shinto is written down

Buddhist scriptures came to Japan written in Chinese. Shinto had no scriptures at that time and there was no way of writing down the Japanese language. By using the Chinese system of writing the Japanese could at last write about Shinto. The emperor encouraged this because Shinto myth made it clear that he was descended from the Sun Goddess and therefore the only rightful ruler (see page 8). Two important histories were written – the *Kojiki* (712 AD) and *Nihonshoki* (720). They tell about the Sun Goddess, the creation of the world and the line of emperors since then.

Shinto and Buddhism

Shinto is basically concerned with making the most of life on earth. It encourages people to respect nature and live in harmony with each other so that they can have pure and useful lives. Shinto ceremonies are usually connected with happy events, like new babies and good harvests.

Buddhism is much more concerned with what happens to people after their life on earth. But people still have to lead good lives in order to be peaceful after death. Although the two religions have been closer to each other at some times than others, most Japanese people feel that they support each other. So it is quite usual for the same person to have a Shinto wedding but a Buddhist funeral. Respect for life, in all its forms, is where the two religions come together.

Zen

Zen is a form of Buddhism that became very popular among *samurai* warriors during the 13th century. Zen stresses the value of meditation. It is a good way of developing a person's powers of concentration and self-control. It gives a person a better understanding of life.

Some Zen teachers recommend meditating about puzzles (*koan*). A *koan* puzzle encourages pupils to think about a problem in a new way. Pupils often have to pretend they are someone or something else in order to solve the puzzle. This helps them to feel what another person is feeling, and to be sympathetic with them. In this way, pupils are closer to achieving the goodness and wisdom of a *bodhisattva*.

Zen monks had a great influence on the development of painting, tea ceremony, flower arranging, drama and landscape gardening because their unusual patterns of thought often led them to look at the world in new and interesting ways (see pages 30 to 31, 33, 39 to 40). Zen Buddhism has become widespread outside Japan this century, especially in the United States and Europe.

▲ *A 19th-century woodblock print of a* samurai *wielding his sword*

Koan puzzles

What is the sound of one hand clapping?

What did your face look like before you were born?

Think and do

1 Read through the last two chapters on Shinto and Buddhism. Now try to describe the differences between the two religions.

2 Why do you think that many Japanese follow both religions?

Key words

meditation thinking calmly

monks men who train to live strict religious lives

sermon a religious talk

sacrifices offerings to a god of killed living things

scholars people who have studied a particular subject very carefully

massacre the killing of many people at the same time

monasteries places where monks live

images pictures

rituals religious ceremonies

Nara – a fixed capital for Japan

Copying the Chinese

Japan's first fixed capital was built at Fujiwara. Three emperors lived there between 694 and 710 AD. Before that the capital had been moved every time an emperor died. People thought it would be unlucky for a new emperor to live where the last one had died.

But by the 7th century the Japanese emperor and his advisors were full of admiration for the way things were done in China. China had a fixed capital, Chang'an (now Xian), where emperors lived one after another. So Japan had to have one. The town plan for Fujiwarakyo was a grid, copied from Chang'an. All the main streets were straight and cut across each other, making a maze of squares.

Fujiwarakyo was completely destroyed by fire in 711. As the capital had just been moved to Nara, the fire may have been deliberate.

Nara – a lively city

Nara was Japan's second fixed capital and a major religious centre. It was the capital only from 710 to 794 AD. At this time Nara had a population of 200,000. The city was very lively, with visitors from China, Korea and, it is said, even as far away as India.

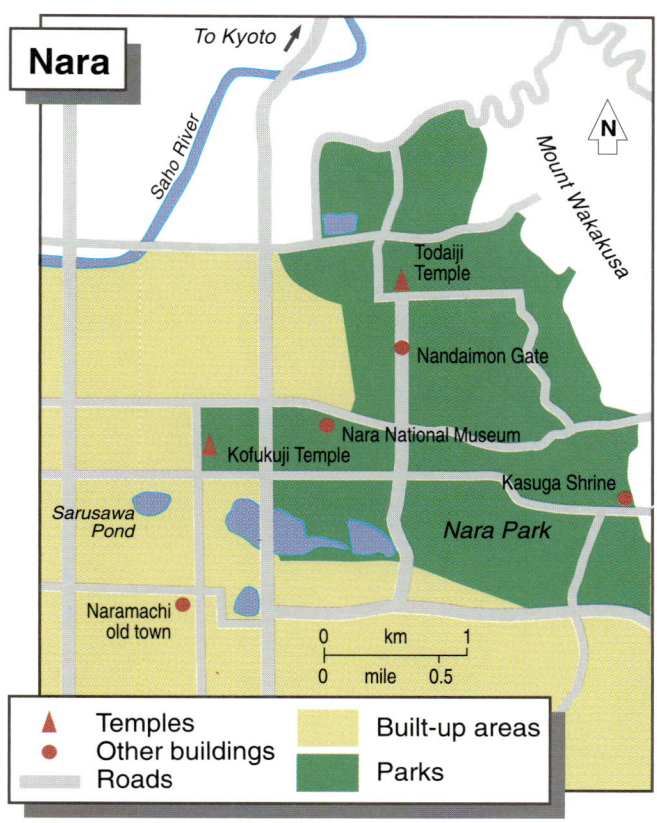

◄ Black ink and brushes are still used in the ancient art of calligraphy

During the period of Nara's glory as the capital of Japan, people were very interested in Buddhism. The city's many beautiful religious buildings and works of art made Nara a symbol of Japan's unity and faith. Chinese influence in art and architecture was also at its height. It is said that during the 8th century AD, Nara had 50 Chinese-style **pagodas**.

Nara – a peaceful city

After the capital was moved to Kyoto, Nara declined. In 1180 it was burned down but the city was soon rebuilt. A hundred years later it was bigger than ever. Today, many travellers enjoy Nara's peaceful streets and old shops. Skilled craftsmen still make the black ink and brushes used for **calligraphy**. The city is also well known for its handmade wooden dolls and fine, sun-bleached linen cloth.

Temples and treasures

Visitors come to Nara to see its historic religious buildings and the wooded park with its many of deer.

Kasuga is a bright, red-painted shrine. It was founded in 709 so that the Shinto gods worshipped there could protect the new city. It has been rebuilt 57 times – roughly every 20 years. Nowadays it is famous for its deer and the 3,000 stone and bronze lanterns that line the pathway to the shrine.

▲ *Deer resting in Nara Park*

▼ *The beautiful red-painted Kasuga Shrine*

◀ *Stone Buddhas clustered together at Kofukuji Temple. Red aprons are the sign of a particular Buddhist group.*

Kofukuji is a Buddhist temple that was controlled by the powerful Fujiwara family. It had a hospital for poor people and Japan's first known **orphanage**. Once it had 175 buildings but now only six remain. Nowadays it is famous for its collection of sculptures. Many of them are over a thousand years old. The reflection of its five-storey pagoda in a nearby pond is one of the famous sights of Nara.

Todaiji was founded by the emperor Shomu (reigned 724 to 49 AD), who became a Buddhist monk. The most important part of this group of buildings is the Great Hall, which is the largest wooden building in the world. It was last rebuilt in 1709; the original was half as big again! Japan's largest statue of Buddha lies inside. It is 15 metres high and was first cast in **bronze** in 752.

◀ *Enormous wooden pillars at Todaiji Temple*

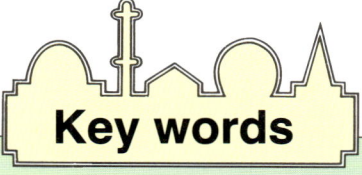

Key words

pagodas decorative towers at Buddhist temples. They were first built in India, where they are called *stupas*; they covered things that belonged to the Buddha Gautama

calligraphy the art of beautiful writing

orphanage a home for children who have no parents

bronze a metal that is a mixture of copper and tin

Shosoin stands in the grounds of Todaiji. It was built of *hinoki* wood (Japanese cypress tree) over 1,200 years ago, as a storehouse for the treasures of Emperor Shomu. Many of these treasures came from other countries such as faraway Persia. Later, other precious items were added to it. The collection of 8,000 items now includes pictures, furniture, ornaments, costumes, armour and musical instruments. Every year some of the treasures are put on show at the Nara National Museum.

Kyoto – the capital of peace

A false start

In 784 AD, Emperor Kanmu decided to move the capital away from Nara because the Buddhist monasteries had become very rich and powerful. They kept interfering in the way he and his advisors tried to govern the country. A site for the new capital was chosen at Nagaoka, but there were many accidents during the building work. After ten years' hard work by 300,000 slaves, and just before the new city was completed, the emperor decided it was an unlucky place and that they should start all over again!

▲ *An old wooden bridge over one of Kyoto's broad rivers*

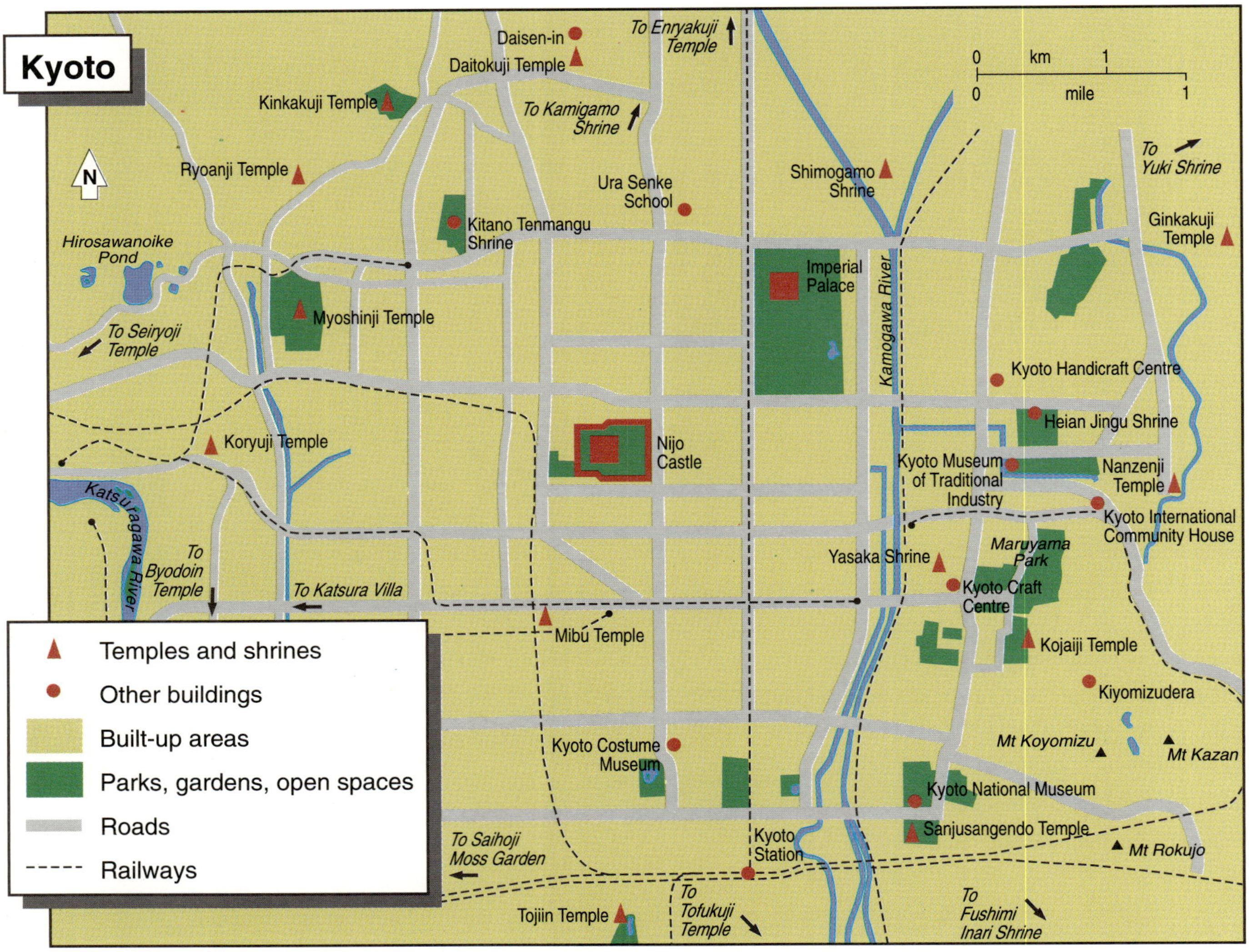

Kyoto

Daisen-in
Daitokuji Temple
To Enryakuji Temple
Kinkakuji Temple
To Kamigamo Shrine
Ryoanji Temple
Ura Senke School
Shimogamo Shrine
To Yuki Shrine
Hirosawanoike Pond
Kitano Tenmangu Shrine
Ginkakuji Temple
Myoshinji Temple
Imperial Palace
To Seiryoji Temple
Kamogawa River
Kyoto Handicraft Centre
Koryuji Temple
Heian Jingu Shrine
Nijo Castle
Kyoto Museum of Traditional Industry
Nanzenji Temple
Katsuragawa River
Kyoto International Community House
To Byodoin Temple
Yasaka Shrine
Maruyama Park
To Katsura Villa
Kyoto Craft Centre
Mibu Temple
Kojaiji Temple
Kiyomizudera
Kyoto Costume Museum
Mt Koyomizu
Mt Kazan
Kyoto National Museum
Roads
To Saihoji Moss Garden
Sanjusangendo Temple
Kyoto Station
Mt Rokujo
Tojiin Temple
To Tofukuji Temple
To Fushimi Inari Shrine

- ▲ Temples and shrines
- ● Other buildings
- Built-up areas
- Parks, gardens, open spaces
- Roads
- - - Railways

The site and the plan

A new site was chosen on a plain ringed by mountains on three sides and watered by the Katsura and Kamo Rivers. The course of the Kamo River was altered to flow around the city. At this time, the Japanese copied many ideas from the Chinese. One of these ideas was that some places were lucky and some were unlucky, and that buildings ought to face in a lucky direction to ward off evil spirits. It was thought that the mountains around Kyoto would protect it from these bad influences.

Like Nara, Kyoto was planned in imitation of the Chinese capital, Chang'an. The basic design was a rectangle 5.2 kilometres from north to south and 4.5 kilometres from east to west. Running down the middle was a grand avenue 85 metres wide. The avenue had two big temples either side of its southern end and the royal palace at the northern end. The city was divided into 1,200 blocks and each street had a stream of fresh water running beside it.

Heian – Kyoto at its height

Kyoto means 'Capital City', but when it was built, the city was known as Heian, 'Capital of Peace and **Tranquillity**'. Emperors reigned over Japan from this city from 794 until 1185.

These centuries are known as the Heian period of Japanese history.

The court at this time was full of life and art. We know a lot about it because courtiers kept diaries and wrote stories about it. One scholar has said, 'Calligraphy was the true religion of the Heian capital.' Poetry was composed, and the world's first novel was written by a woman, Lady Murasaki Shikibu. More unusual arts were colour-matching and **incense**-burning competitions! The emperors themselves spent a lot of their time taking part in religious ceremonies.

After this exciting period, power fell from the emperors and their advisors into the hands of *shoguns* (warlords), who ruled from Kamakura until 1333 (see map on page 7). Then, Kyoto became the seat of government again for the next 200 years, but the Ashikaga *shoguns* were very weak. After 1600, Japan was ruled from Edo, the city that was renamed Tokyo (Eastern Capital) in 1868. But throughout this time, Kyoto remained the spiritual and cultural capital of Japan.

After the glory

By the 9th century, Kyoto had a population of 100,000. About 10,000 of these were courtiers

▼ *Drama developed during the Heian period. In this wood block print, an actor wields an axe at his victim.*

and officials. The rest of the workers were servants, craftsmen and merchants who made it possible for these palace officials to live in luxury.

By the 10th century, the government had become so weak that bandits had made the city anything but a place of peace. Large areas of the city were never built up. Fire remained a permanent curse. After a third major blaze destroyed the emperor's Great Audience Hall in 1156, it was not rebuilt.

In 1467, a huge civil war broke out. Bands of **samurai** fought one another. Each one wanted to make their own leader *shogun*. Within ten years almost all of Kyoto had been burned to the ground. The wars went on for over a hundred years. Most of Kyoto's older buildings that can be seen today were put up after 1600, when the Tokugawa family finally established a strong government and the country was peaceful again.

▼ *Old homes and shops in Kyoto*

▲ *A modern street scene in Kyoto. Some people are still wearing traditional dress.*

Modern Kyoto

After Tokyo became the capital in 1868, Kyoto changed at a slower pace than the new city. Tokyo soon had a railway and modern western-style buildings. In 1923, though, much of Tokyo was destroyed by a great earthquake which killed 140,000 people. It was almost all burned down again by bombing in 1945. Kyoto was spared these great disasters.

Now, Kyoto does have many glistening new buildings, including a striking conference centre. Sometimes, visitors arriving at the main railway station are disappointed at first, because so many of the buildings look very modern. But Kyoto is a city the visitor has to get to know from the inside – walking into temples, strolling around their gardens and exploring the city's side streets. Their calm and quiet are a peaceful haven.

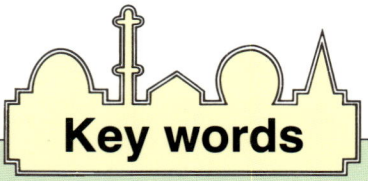

Key words

tranquillity calm quiet

incense sweet-smelling wood, burned to give out its perfume

samurai warriors

Palaces of splendour

Kyoto was the home of the emperor and his court for many centuries, so the city had a lot of palace buildings. Here, the country's rulers could live, work, rest and amuse themselves. Because Kyoto has suffered so much from fires and wars over the years, very few of these buildings remain. Those that do have often been rebuilt, though usually in a style and with materials as close as possible to the original. These are some of the most outstanding.

Impressive palaces

The Imperial Palace The Emperor of Japan now lives in Tokyo. But the Imperial Palace in Kyoto is always used for the ceremonies that are performed when a new emperor comes to the throne. These ceremonies last several days and are one of the very few times when the emperor wears traditional court costume rather than western-style clothes.

The first ceremony takes place in front of the shrines in the palace. Here, it is declared that the heir to the throne has become the new emperor. In the second ceremony, the new emperor formally takes the throne. The third is called the 'Great Food Offering Ritual'. The rice offered to the Sun Goddess (see page 8) at this ceremony is grown in two holy fields, east and west of Kyoto. The last time these ceremonies were held was in November 1990 when Emperor Akihito came to the throne.

The palace moved to its present site in 1790. The buildings date from 1855, replacing earlier ones destroyed by fire. They are built in the Heian style of a thousand years ago (see page 21). The palace grounds cover 11.3 hectares.

The fortress with a squeaky floor Nijo Castle is an imposing fortress surrounded by a moat. The castle was begun in 1569 and was used by the *shogun* when he came to visit the emperor. It has a special squeaky floor called the 'nightingale floor'. This was put in to warn the *shogun's* guards of possible **assassins** coming into the castle by night.

▼ *Paintings on the inside walls of the Imperial Palace*

Elegant Katsura Imperial Villa This grand residence was built as a country retreat on the west bank of the Katsura river. Its plain, simple lines make it look extremely modern, but it is almost 400 years old. Many western architects have been influenced by this building. It is surrounded by a tranquil garden and faces on to an artificial boating pond which reflects the outline of the villa.

Palace gardens Shugakuin Detached Palace was also built as a country retreat about 350 years ago. It is located in the foothills of Mount Hiei, to the north-east of the city. Its most famous feature is the way its gardens, the largest in Kyoto, have been designed to use the surrounding hills as a background. Japanese call this effect 'borrowed scenery'.

Palaces as Temples

Palaces of gold and silver Kinkakuji is also known as the 'Golden Pavilion'. It is probably the most famous building in all Kyoto. The building is now a Zen temple. It was built around 1400 as a residence for Yoshimitsu, the third of the Ashikaga *shoguns* (see page 21).

▲ *The Chinese Gate at Nijo, showing the Chinese influence in its shape and decoration*

▶*The Golden Pavilion surrounded by gardens*

Kinkakuji was restored after damage in the Onin war of 1467-77, and miraculously escaped a fire which gutted surrounding buildings in 1565. In 1950 it was completely destroyed by **arson**. The famous writer, Mishima Yukio, wrote a novel about this strange event, called *The Temple of the Golden Pavilion*.

The present building is an exact **replica** of the original and was completed in 1955. It is a mixture of styles and influences, with a hall on the ground floor that is dedicated to the Amida Buddha. A hall built for Kannon, the Goddess of Mercy, is on the first floor. A Chinese-style room sits on the top!

There is also a 'Silver Pavilion' (Ginkakuji), built by another Ashikaga *shogun* in 1489. The building is rather a surprise, as it does not look silver at all! The *shogun* wanted it covered with **silver-leaf**, but he died before this was done. Nevertheless the name stuck. Outside, the garden has a flat-topped cone of fine white sand, like a volcano.

The temple with the tigers!
Nanzenji is now the head temple of one of the sects of Zen Buddhism, but it was first built as a home for a retired emperor. The temple is famous for its paintings of tigers, but the artist had only seen a tiger-skin!

The temple of the phoenix
Byodoin is now a temple as well, but it began as a country house for a member of the powerful Fujiwara family. It is located at Uji, outside Kyoto, in the middle of a tea-growing district. It was converted to a temple in 1052-3.

The building became known as **Phoenix Hall** because its ground plan looks like the outline of a phoenix, a legendary bird that is a symbol of rebirth and good fortune. There are also two bronze phoenixes on the roof.

Inside, there is a huge statue of Buddha carved by the great **sculptor**, Jocho, around 1200. It is the only one of his works known to have survived. The Middle Hall of the building represents Amida's Pure Land –

▲ *The Byodoin Temple*

a Buddhist heaven. Byodoin is one of the greatest masterpieces of Heian period architecture.

Key words

assassin a person who is paid to commit murder

arson a fire that has been started on purpose

replica a copy of something

silver-leaf silver that is beaten into thin leaves

phoenix a mythical bird that is reborn out of the ashes of its own nest

sculptor someone who makes statues or carvings

Temples and shrines

Kyoto has over 1,600 Buddhist temples and about 300 Shinto shrines. Many have stories and myths attached to them. These are a few of the most famous and interesting houses of worship.

Tales of Buddhist temples

The Temple of Clear Water Kiyomizudera means 'Temple of Clear Water'. Its main hall has a spectacular verandah jutting out from the steep hillside on which the temple is built. When Japanese people have to take a risky decision, they call it 'jumping from Kiyomizu'! The pathway up to the temple is lined with so many souvenir shops that visitors have called it 'Teapot Lane'.

▲ A wooden temple guardian frightens evil spirits.

▼ Kiyomizudera Temple at autumn time

Praying for mercy Sanjusangendo Temple was first built in 1164 and rebuilt in 1266. It has 1,001 statues of Kannon, the Goddess of Mercy. The main one was carved by the sculptor Tankei when he was 82 years old. Japanese students often go to a Kannon temple at examination time to pray for her help.

The tallest pagoda Tojiin Temple dates from 796 and its pagoda, last rebuilt in 1644, is the tallest in Japan (60 metres). In the beautiful garden stands the tomb of the *shoguns* of the Ashikaga family.

The warriors' temple Enryakuji Temple is set in a deep forest of cedar trees on Mount Hiei. Some of the most famous leaders of Japanese Buddhism were trained here. At one time it was so rich and powerful that it had 3,000 buildings and an army of warrior monks. The warlord, Oda Nobunaga, thought it was much too powerful and burned it down in 1571. The monks never interfered in politics again.

▶ *The goddess Kannon*

Stories of Shinto shrines
The shrine of the scholar Kitano Tenmangu Shrine honours the memory of a great scholar and poet called Sugiwara no Michizane. He became a close friend of the emperor, which made the powerful Fujiwara family jealous. They accused him of plotting against the emperor and had him sent to the far-off southern island of Kyushu, where he died. After his death in 903 Kyoto began to suffer from fires, storms and earthquakes. It was thought that these were caused by Michizane's angry ghost. The Kitano shrine was built to beg the ghost's forgiveness.

The shrine to the God of Rice Fushimi Inari Taisha Shrine is named after Inari, the Shinto *kami* who takes care of rice and other grains. For rice-farmers especially, he was a very important god. His messenger was a white fox who could change into a human being.

This shrine is at the foot of Mount Inari and is the most important of 40,000 other shrines that honour Inari. In the grounds of the shrine there are hundreds of statues of foxes. Ten thousand red-painted arches (*torii*) line a 4 kilometre path that leads up to it.

▶ *An avenue of torii leading up to Fushimi Inari Taisha Shrine*

▼ *Fox statues at Fushimi Inari Taisha Shrine. Notice the white fortune slip tied to a fox's ear. Visitors to shrines buy fortune slips which tell them what their luck will be in the future.*

The art of gardening

Japanese gardens are works of art. Designers of famous gardens are thought of as great artists, just like painters or sculptors. Temples and palaces often have beautiful gardens because a garden is a place for deep religious thought. Most gardens in Kyoto are influenced by the ideas of Zen Buddhism (see page 16).

One of the most famous garden designers was Kobori Enshu (1579-1647), who was also a poet, architect and expert on calligraphy, pottery and tea ceremony. Only a few examples of his work are left, all in Kyoto. One is at Nanzenji, where the tiger-paintings are (see page 26). Another is at Daitokuji temple, where the warlord Oda Nobunaga is buried. Lady Murasaki Shikibu, who wrote *The Tale of Genji*, is also said to be buried in one of the gardens there (see page 21).

In western countries, flowers are usually the most important feature of a garden. In Japan, rocks, water, trees and shrubs are usually more important than flowers. Sometimes, Japanese gardens also have stone bridges, fountains and lanterns. Large goldfish or carp swim in the ponds. An unusually-shaped rock can remind Japanese people of a lucky creature, such as a tortoise, a crane, a tiger or a dragon.

Specially-built houses for tea ceremony (see page 39) are often built in gardens. An elegant garden puts people in a calm frame of mind. Tea ceremony and peaceful gardens express many of the ideas in Zen.

Gardens for the gods

In ancient times, Japanese people thought that the Shinto *kami* (see page 10) lived in dense clumps of trees, in places sheltered by rings of rocks or in areas protected by surrounding streams. Trees, rocks and water are valued by Japanese gardeners.

▼ *A typical garden for the Shinto* kami *with rocks, shrubs, trees and water, which is full of Koi carp*

Gardens of moss and rocks

Kyoto probably has more famous and unusual gardens than any other city in the world.

At Saihoji, a Zen temple, there is a garden that features a hundred kinds of moss. In most western countries gardeners usually think of moss as ugly or a nuisance. But Japanese people like moss because it shows the effect that time and weather have on wood or stones. Thick, bright green moss growing on trees and rocks reminds people how old these natural things are. The moss garden at Saihoji is especially beautiful after a shower of rain, when the rich green mosses sparkle with light reflected through drops of water.

▲ *People meditate peacefully by the garden at Ryoanji.*

Streams of stones

Kyoto is the home of a kind of garden that is only found in Japan. It is known as *karesansui*, which means 'mountain stream without water'. These gardens consist of rocks and sand or gravel, designed to look like a river winding its way through mountains to the ocean.

One of the best of these stone gardens surrounds the home of the **abbot** at Daisen-in, part of the Daitokuji Temple. White gravel is used to look like a powerful waterfall forcing its way through high peaks. Another famous example of *karesansui* can be seen at Ryoanji Temple, where a walled garden consists simply of raked white sand and 15 rugged rocks, placed like islands in an ocean.

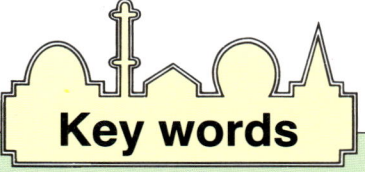

Think and do

You can make your own miniature Japanese garden. Fill an old plastic bowl or a seed tray with soil, placing some stones at the bottom to help with drainage. Read through the chapter on gardens and decide which type of garden you wish to make. All you need is some moss, large stones, gravel for making a false river, and some twigs which can be used as trees. The pictures of Japanese gardens should help to show the peaceful mood that they create.

Key words

abbot the leading monk in a monastery

Dance and drama

Dancing and religion

An important part of the myth in which the Sun Goddess, Amaterasu, brought light back into the world, is when she came out of the cave to join in the dancing (see page 8). So dance is a vital part of Japanese tradition.

Dances called *kagura* were performed at Shinto shrines each year to call on the *kami* (gods) to come down among ordinary people. The dancers often wore masks and rich costumes. The music came from **zithers**, flutes and wooden clappers, and sometimes the dancers sang.

Songs and dances were also performed at rice-planting time, in the hope that they would help bring a good harvest. Singing and dancing are still carried out at village festivals (*matsuri*) in the spring and autumn.

▼ *Children dressed in traditional costume play drums at the Tanabata (Star) Festival in Kyoto.*

◀ A No actor performs with his fan and mask

No

No is a kind of drama that began in the 14th century in Kyoto. It has ancient religious origins. The actors are all men, although they play women's parts as well. Some actors wear masks. They chant their words and move very slowly and deliberately as they act. A No actor always has one heel on the ground. They wear gorgeous costumes, sometimes up to five layers! Musicians with flutes and drums sit beside the stage.

The stories for No plays often come from early legends and famous ancient writings. They were then influenced by Zen Buddhist thought. Tales of ghosts, gods and demons are performed, as well as stories about men and women. Buddhist ideas about rebirth mean that characters can sometimes change completely during a play. A woman can turn into a snake and a *samurai* into a butterfly!

There is almost no scenery except a painted back drop. Actors hold fans in different positions to suggest a dagger, a lantern or even a rising moon. Fans also help explain actions such as listening or sleeping.

Troupes of No actors were originally employed by temples and shrines. They performed at religious festivals to teach and entertain ordinary people. The greatest masters of No were Kan'ami and his son Zeami, who wrote over 40 plays. The *shogun* gave these great artists his support. No is still performed by a small number of professional actors today. They are usually the sons of other No actors and begin their training at the age of seven.

In June, No drama can be seen outside Kyoto's Heian shrine, by the light of flaring torches, which add an eerie atmosphere.

Comedy acts!

No plays were often rather frightening, or sometimes solemn and sad. So short comic sketches were sometimes put on between one No play and the next. These short breaks are called *kyogen*, which means 'crazy words'! They often poke fun at important people. *Kyogen* can be seen at Mibu Temple in Kyoto every April. The parts are played by local people who worship at the temple. *Kyogen* has been performed here for over 600 years.

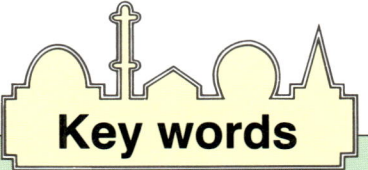

Key words

zither a flat, wooden musical instrument with between 29 and 42 metal strings that are plucked

Festivals and fun

Kyoto is home to some of Japan's most colourful festivals. There is a festival of some sort in almost every month of the year. These are some of the most important.

New Year's luck

On New Year's Day, January 1st, Buddhist temples and Shinto shrines throughout Kyoto are crowded with families in their best clothes. Even families that are not particularly religious think it brings good luck to visit a house of worship at the beginning of the year.

▲ *Pilgrims make their way to the Fushimi Inara Taisha Shrine on New Year's Day.*

The bean-scattering festival

February 3rd marks the festival of Setsubun. It was originally a New Year's custom in the traditional Chinese calendar. People celebrate by throwing beans around their houses or at temples. This is meant to drive out evil spirits and mark the end of the coldest part of winter.

A festival of fire

On March 15th a fire festival is held at Seiryoji Temple to mark the anniversary of the death of Buddha Gautama. Three huge pine torches, each 6 metres long, are burned. The way they burn is supposed to tell how good the coming year's harvest will be.

Spring celebration

April is the month for admiring the colourful cherry blossom, which marks the coming of spring. There are 20 different places in Kyoto that are famous for their cherry blossom. Maruyama Park, to the east of the Yasaka Shrine, is particularly beautiful at this time of year.

◄ *Making one of the torches for the fire festival at Seiryoji Temple*

The Aoi festival of thanks

On May 15th every year, 300 people put on costumes of the Heian period and join a procession of ox carts. Together, they go to the two Kamo shrines, Shimogamo and Kamigamo, where people thank the gods for protecting their city. The special hats that are worn, and the carts, are decorated with hollyhocks and leaves of the wild ginger plant. In Japanese, hollyhocks are called *aoi*, which gives the festival its name.

On the third Sunday in May, people hold boating parties, in memory of the parties held by emperors during the Heian period. Richly decorated boats float down the Oi River, with musicians and dancers to entertain the guests.

The Gion festival of hope

The Gion festival lasts for a whole month through June and July. The high point of the festival comes on July 17th, with a procession of wagons from the Yasaka Shrine. The wagons carry musicians, or people dressed up as famous figures from history or legend. Some of the wagons weigh up to 12 tonnes!

The festival began in 869 AD, when a terrible plague was killing hundreds of Kyoto's citizens. In desperation, the people paraded every holy image and **relic** they could find in the hope that one of the gods would save them.

▼ *An ox pulls a cart decorated with hollyhocks at the Aoi Festival.*

The O-bon festival of the dead

August 16th is the day of O-bon, a festival to remember the dead. A huge bonfire is lit on Mount Daimonjiyama on the eastern edge of the city. Pine branches are laid out in the shape of the Chinese character '*dai*', which means 'great'. At sunset, the branches are set alight to say goodbye to the souls of the dead as they return to heaven at the end of the festival. The blaze can be seen from all over Kyoto.

▲ *A tall wagon carrying musicians from the Yasaka Shrine at the Gion Festival*

A celebration of history

Every year, Kyoto celebrates the time when the city was the capital of the whole of Japan. On October 22nd at the Yuki Shrine in Kurama, a village north of Kyoto, two **portable** shrines (*mikoshi*) are paraded by torchlight, and torches are carried around the grounds right through the night.

On the same day, a much bigger event called Jidai, or the Festival of the Ages, takes place. It is held at the Heian Shrine. The festival began in 1895 when the shrine was built to mark the 1100th anniversary of the founding of Kyoto. It is a small replica of the first Imperial Palace built by Emperor Kanmu in 794 AD. The main event of the festival is a procession of people dressed up as famous figures from Japanese history.

A festival for children

On August 23rd to 24th, children play games and have parties in honour of Jizo, the Buddhist god who keeps children safe.

A healthy New Year!

On New Year's Eve a fire of okera herbs is lit at the Yasaka Shrine. Visitors can take home lengths of tarred rope lit from this fire. If they use these to light the fire that cooks the first meal of the New Year, it is thought that the family will be protected from illness.

Think and do

Many Japanese festivals use light or fire. How many festivals do you celebrate or know of where light, fire, or materials for making fire are used? What is the importance of light or fire in each festival?

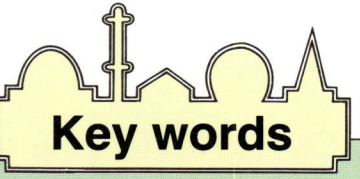

Key words

relic a piece of a dead holy person's body or belongings, thought to be sacred

portable describes something that can be carried easily

The art of cooking

Kyoto has its own special style of cooking. It is a combination of three very different traditions: the dishes served to the ancient court nobility, the dainty snacks served before tea ceremony and the vegetarian dishes preferred by Buddhist monks. Japanese cooking is becoming very popular in western countries because it is healthy, tasty and very attractively presented.

Pleasing to the eye

Food for the nobility was arranged to look as beautiful as possible. The dishes were supposed to balance each other out. This tradition developed into a basic pattern for all Japanese meals: soup with three side-dishes, usually one of raw sea-food, one of grilled fowl or fish and another of something that has been gently boiled. A grand banquet

▲ *A restaurant displays its dishes.*

in this style might consist of three soups and 11 side dishes. This very formal style of cooking is still used at feasts held for weddings and funerals.

▼ *A bamboo dish of* tempura *– seafood and vegetables flash-fried in a light, crisp batter*

Snacks before tea

The meal served before tea ceremony starts with small snacks, followed by soup, pickles, rice, sweets and fruit. *Sake*, a colourless wine made from rice, is served during the meal. Tea is drunk afterwards.

Healthy eating

Buddhist monks are forbidden to eat meat, so they have developed their own vegetarian style of cookery. Vegetable oils are used instead of animal fats for frying food. For protein, soybeans are eaten, especially in the form of *tofu*. *Tofu* is made by boiling the beans and separating out the liquid from the pulp, which looks rather like white blancmange. *Tofu* is cheap, low in fat, high in protein and easy to digest. It can be fried, put in soups and stews instead of meat, or eaten hot or chilled with sauces, spices, chopped onions or soy sauce. *Tofu* is healthy and it can be delicious!

▼ *Making* sake *from cooked rice*

▲ *Roasted* tai *fish for sale. They are eaten at the New Year celebration.*

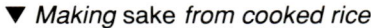

Two Japanese arts

Kyoto is the home of two famous Japanese arts: tea ceremony and flower arranging. Both are influenced by Buddhist thinking. Tea came to Japan from China, as did many other goods, ideas and crafts. But the Japanese people have always used them in their own special way.

Tea ceremony

Tea was used as a medicine long before it was drunk for pleasure. Monks began to use it to help them stay awake during long hours of meditation. Naturally, they prepared the tea in a slow and careful way so that the calm mood needed for meditation was not disturbed. In time, they found that their slow, peaceful way of making tea brought them some of the same benefits that the meditation itself offered: a sense of being quite calm, but alert at the same time.

The formal tea ceremony (*chanoyu*) was perfected by Sen No Rikyu, 400 years ago. Sen No Rikyu insisted that it was not necessary to have expensive pottery or splendid surroundings to perform tea ceremony. It was perhaps even more suitable to use a plain iron kettle, rough country-style bowls, a water-dipper and a whisk made from bamboo, and linen cloths for wiping the bowls.

▲ *A painting of a Japanese tea ceremony in the late 19th century*

◀ *A Japanese tea ceremony today. Notice the simple pots and flower arrangement.*

Performing tea ceremony

The ideal host prepares everything carefully beforehand, and takes great trouble over little details, like splashing the approach to the tea house with water, so that all the shrubs and the pathway look bright and fresh. The host should also be careful to invite guests who get along well with one another.

Before entering the actual tea room, guests should rinse their hands and mouths with fresh water, just as they do on entering a Shinto shrine. While tea is being prepared and served, the conversation should be about the tea being served and the bowls that are used. It can also be about the vase of flowers and the hanging-scroll with a painting or a poem on it, which are the only correct decorations for the plain tea room. The flowers and scroll should be chosen to suit the time of day and the season of the year.

People attending tea ceremony always kneel down on woven straw mats called *tatami*. There are no tables, as the tea cups and plates of sugar cakes are placed on the floor in front of each guest. A full-length tea ceremony, including the meal which is eaten before it, can last four hours or even longer.

Flower arranging

Japanese flower arranging is called *ikebana*, which means 'living flowers'. This art goes back to the time when Buddhism was first introduced into Japan. A vase of flowers was placed in front of the statue of Buddha as an offering. The flowers were arranged so that the main stem was one-and-a-half times as high as the vase it was put in. This main stem was set upright at the centre of the arrangement. An additional stem was placed either side of it.

This custom of placing simple, balanced arrangements as an offering continued until 1462. Then, a flower arranger called Senkei introduced a new style in which flowers and branches were used to suggest a whole landscape of hills, valleys and waterfalls, rather like some Japanese gardens.

By the 18th century, Senkei's idea had been developed and turned into a system of rules for one particular style of flower arranging. This style uses nine branches, centred on one which is three to five times as high as its container. All the other branches are chosen and arranged with the central branch in mind. Each branch has a job to do, supporting or balancing the others, giving depth or breadth to the whole arrangement or covering up the point where they all meet.

This, of course, was only one style among many. A much simpler style was developed by Sen No Rikyu to go with tea ceremony. His arrangements sometimes consisted of only a single flower or branch. The most popular style of *ikebana* followed nowadays, divides the arrangement into three main parts. These stand for earth, heaven and man. There are 3,000 *ikebana* schools in Japan with over 15,000,000 students. The wives of many American officers stationed in Japan in 1945, after World War Two, spread the knowledge of *ikebana* to western countries.

▲ *A simple* ikebana *flower arrangement*

The crafts of Kyoto

Kyoto has an ancient tradition of craftsmanship. It grew out of the need to supply the emperor's court and the city's wealthy monasteries with gorgeous robes, statues, paintings and objects for use in ceremonies. Later on, the many pilgrims, scholars and merchants who visited the city offered a wider market for Kyoto wares.

▲ *Kyoto is famous for its embroidered textiles.*

Colourful cloth

Kyoto is famous for its stunning textiles produced by the dyeing method known as *yuzen*. This was invented by a fan painter called Miyazaki Yuzen. The first step in the process is to paint a fine outline of the design on to the cloth using a tracing fluid. This is made from the natural sap of a plant that the Japanese called *tsuyukusa*. The outline is then covered with a sticky paste made from rice. Soybean milk is then spread over the cloth to prevent dyes from running into one another.

When the paste and milk have dried, the designs are brushed in with different coloured dyes. Then the coloured parts are covered with more rice paste to protect them during the next step, when the background colour dye is brushed in. The dyes are then fixed into the cloth by steaming. Finally, the cloth is rinsed in running water until all the tracing fluid and rice paste have been washed out. Further decoration is sometimes embroidered on to the cloth.

The main advantage of the *yuzen* method of dyeing is that it can be used to produce incredibly detailed designs. But it takes great skill from the craftsman – and a lot of cash from the customer!

Perfect pots

Pottery has been made in the Kyoto area since the 8th century AD. At first, the pots were mostly plain green. Later, potters learned how to decorate them with glazes of red, gold and brown. Many of the finest bowls and plates were made for tea ceremony (see page 39). Each year, between August 7th and 10th, a pottery festival is held in Kyoto's Gojo Street, where stallholders sell all kinds of pottery at bargain prices.

▶ *A 17th-century tea-leaf jar with red, gold and brown glazes*

Shiny enamel

Another celebrated Kyoto craft is enamelling. Fine metal wires are first fixed to a metal surface to create a pattern. Different-coloured glossy enamels can then be poured into the patterned shapes. They are then fired in an oven to make them solid. The surface is smoothed to a brilliant shine by grinding and polishing. This technique has been used to decorate door handles, sword hilts, locks and brush holders.

▲ *Sword scabbards enamelled in red, gold and black*

Layers of lacquer

Lacquering is a craft that the Japanese originally learned from China. The Japanese craftsmen became so good at it that in English-speaking countries lacquering was often known as 'Japanning'.

Lacquer is made from the sticky sap of a tree that the Japanese call *urushi*. The lacquer can be used both to stick things together and to coat items with a heat-resistant varnish.

This is often coloured for decoration and polished to a brilliant shine.

Lacquer also seeps into **porous** materials, such as wood and unglazed earthenware. This seals them so that they can be used for holding liquids. Not only wood and pottery have been lacquered, but also items made of bamboo, leather and metal. Some *samurai* used to wear helmets made of lacquered leather. These were not only light and tough, but waterproof as well.

The natural colour of lacquer is a reddish-brown, but Japanese craftsmen learned how to make it black, yellow and green. To get a really deep shine on a lacquered object it is necessary to build up many layers of lacquer. This obviously takes a long time, and is expensive. Thickly-lacquered objects can have a design carved into them, or they can be inlaid with a precious metal or **mother-of-pearl**. Great care must be taken not to get any dust on the lacquered object while it is drying or the effect will be ruined.

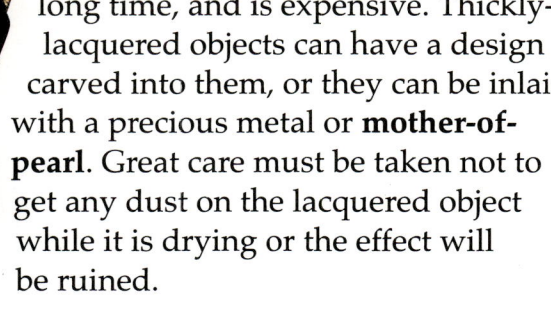

◄ *Lacquered boxes – inro – with inlaid decoration*

One of the most famous types of lacquer decoration is named after Kyoto's Kodaiji Temple. It was first made in the late 1500s and usually shows flowers or elegant sprays of grasses. These are made of speckles of real gold and silver against a black background.

Boxes, bowls, trays, chests and small tables are often lacquered. Lacquered goods are not only beautiful but very hard wearing.

Fine fans

Fans were introduced to Japan from China in the 8th century. Japan's sticky summer climate makes it a relief to have a fan for keeping cool. But they soon became objects of fashion for both men and women. The first fans were stiff and flat, but by about 900 AD the Japanese had invented the folding fan. This was much harder to damage and could be carried conveniently in the sleeve of a **kimono**.

Fans are usually made of bamboo covered with paper. They can be decorated with designs, pictures or even with poems. *Samurai* leaders used to carry iron fans in battle to make signals to their troops. Dancers held them to make the movements of their arms seem more graceful. Fans are used by actors in No plays (see page 33). Nowadays, a brightly-decorated fan is often bought as a souvenir.

Piles of paper

Paper was introduced from Korea around 600 AD. When the emperor's government settled down permanently at Nara, it kept more written records of taxes, grants of land, and other facts and figures. At the same time, the growth of Buddhism meant that many more people wanted to study the Buddhist scriptures. Both these developments created a great demand for paper.

Documents dating from this period survive in the Shosoin (see page 19). They are written on more than 230 different types of paper.

The art of paper making reached even greater heights when the capital moved to Kyoto. Courtiers had multi-coloured, gold-speckled paper specially made for writing poetry on. In 806, the government set up its own official paper mill beside the Kamiyagawa River in Kyoto. The mill even produced recycled paper made from paper that had already been written on. As it was difficult to get the ink out, the recycled paper was pale grey in colour.

In Japan, paper is not only used for stationery and books, but also for making fans and lanterns. It often covers internal walls and sliding doors. Nowadays, the small town of Ayabe, outside Kyoto, remains a leading centre for making fine hand-crafted paper.

◀ Fans are a favourite souvenir from Kyoto.

▲ *A ceremonial doll with traditional musicians*

Dolls for all

Dolls have not just been used as toys. In Shinto rituals, paper dolls were ceremonially thrown away. This helped people to feel cleansed. Buddhist monks also used dolls as teaching aids.

Kyoto is famous for two kinds of doll: 'palace dolls' and 'grooved dolls'. 'Palace dolls', in the shape of chubby baby boys, were traditionally given to guests of the emperor. 'Grooved dolls' are made from the wood of willow trees, and grooved so that the dolls' costumes can be neatly tucked into the grooves. The result looks very realistic. These dolls were first made at the Kamo shrines in the 1730s, from left-over scraps of wood and cloth.

Each year, on March 3rd, girls all over Japan celebrate the Dolls Festival. They set up displays of elaborately costumed dolls, which represent an emperor and an empress and their courtiers, musicians and guards.

Culture and the future

The crafts of Kyoto, as well as the beautiful old buildings, ancient traditions, festivals and arts are still very important to the people of Japan. The fast pace of modern life has not destroyed the old ways. This is partly because most of the traditions are closely tied to Shinto and Buddhism, which are so important in Japan. Kyoto is seen as Japan's religious and cultural centre. It is hard to think this will ever change.

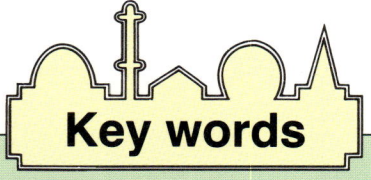

Key words

porous able to absorb liquids

mother-of-pearl the shiny, rainbow-coloured inner surface of some sea shells

kimono the wide-sleeved traditional Japanese dress

Important events in Japanese history

The following are some important events with the dates on which they occurred:

BC BEFORE THE BIRTH OF CHRIST
660 The traditional date when the first Emperor, Jinmu, began to rule

AD AFTER THE BIRTH OF CHRIST
400 The leaders of the Yamato area possibly began to rule Japan around this time
552 The traditional date for the introduction of Buddhism into Japan from China
587 Soga family, supporters of Buddhism, become powerful
607 Prince Shotoku builds Horyuji temple and monastery
694 Fujiwara is built as the first fixed capital of Japan
710 The capital is moved to Nara
712 Publication of the *Kojiki* (Record of Ancient Matters)
720 Publication of *Nihon Shoki* (Chronicle of Japan)
741 Emperor Shomu orders each province to build Buddhist monasteries
752 Emperor Shomu dedicates the Great Buddha (Daibutsu) at Nara
784 A new capital is built at Nagaoka
794 The capital is moved to Kyoto
1000 Around this time the Tale of Genji, a novel about a prince, is written by Lady Murasaki Shikibu
1192 Kamakura becomes the real centre of government
1338 The Ashikaga family become *shoguns*

1467–77 The Onin war marks the beginning of more than a century of conflict
1543 The first Europeans arrive
1600 The Tokugawa family defeat their rivals to become *shoguns*
1636–39 Japan ends contacts with foreign countries. Christianity is banned
1853 An American fleet under Commodore Perry forces Japan to open trade
1867–68 The Tokugawa family of *shoguns* is overthrown
1868–1912 The capital is shifted from Kyoto to Edo, which is renamed Tokyo
1872 Japan's first railway is opened
1873 Christianity is permitted again
1889 Japan adopts a western-style government
1894–95 Japan defeats China and takes over the island of Taiwan
1902 Japan becomes an ally of Britain
1905 Japan defeats Russia in war
1910 Japan takes over Korea
1923 The Great Kanto earthquake destroys much of Tokyo
1931 The Japanese army begins to take over northern China
1937 Japan invades China
1941 Japan enters World War Two
1945 Atomic bombs dropped on Hiroshima and Nagasaki
1945–52 Japan is occupied by American troops
1958 Japan launches the world's largest oil tanker
1960–70s Japan becomes a major industrial country
1989 Emperor Hirohito dies
1990 Emperor Akihito is crowned

Further reading

For younger readers
The Buddhist World Ann Bancroft (Macdonald)
On the Map: Japan Daphne Butler (Simon
& Schuster)
Great Civilizations: Japan Mavis Pilbeam (Watts)
Samurai Warriors Jenny Roberts (Watts)
Passport to Japan Richard Tames (Watts)

For older readers
The Cambridge Encyclopaedia of Japan
Richard Bowring & Peter Kornicki (Cambridge
University Press)
The Cultural Atlas of Japan Martin Collcutt,
Marius Jansen & Isao Kamakura (Phaidon)
The Living Arts of Japan John Reeve (British
Museum Publications)
A Traveller's History of Japan Richard Tames
(Windrush Press)

Index